TEAM TIME MACHINE
ADDS TO THE
BILL OF RIGHTS

BY THERESE M. SHEA

Gareth Stevens
PUBLISHING

Please visit our website, www.garethstevens.com. For a free color catalog of all our high-quality books, call toll free 1-800-542-2595 or fax 1-877-542-2596.

Library of Congress Cataloging-in-Publication Data

Names: Shea, Therese, author.
Title: Team time machine adds to the Bill of Rights / Therese M Shea.
Description: New York : Gareth Stevens Publishing, 2021. | Series: Team
    time machine: the new nation | Includes index.
Identifiers: LCCN 2019055662 | ISBN 9781538257012 (library binding) | ISBN
    9781538256992 (paperback) | ISBN 9781538257005 (6 Pack) | ISBN 9781538257029
    (ebook)
Subjects: LCSH: United States. Constitution. 1st–10th Amendments–Juvenile
    literature. | Civil rights–United States–Juvenile literature.
Classification: LCC KF4750 .S523 2020 | DDC 342.7308/5–dc23
LC record available at https://lccn.loc.gov/2019055662

First Edition

Published in 2021 by
Gareth Stevens Publishing
111 East 14th Street, Suite 349
New York, NY 10003

Designer: Katelyn E. Reynolds
Editor: Therese Shea

Photo credits: Cover, p. 1 Bettmann/Getty Images; cover, pp. 1–24 (series characters) Lorelyn Medina/Shutterstock.com; cover, pp. 1–24 (time machine elements) Agor2012/Shutterstock.com; cover, pp. 1–24 (background texture) somen/Shutterstock.com; p. 5 GordonsLife/iStock/Getty Images Plus; p. 7 Thiranun Kunatum/Shutterstock.com; p. 9 Cornelius Tiebout, artist and engraver of the original; this copy engraved by Hatch & Smillie and printed by J. &. G. Neale/Vzeebjtf/Wikipedia.org; p. 11 © CORBIS/Corbis via Getty Images; p. 13 (main) courtesy of the Library of Congress; p. 13 (inset) Original authors were the barons and King John of England/EarthsoundWikipedia.org; p. 15 © iStockphoto.com/StephanieCraig; p. 17 Karl_Sonnenberg/Shutterstock.com; p. 19 Andrey_Kuzmin/Shutterstock.com; p. 21 Ron Chapple/The Image Bank/Getty Images Plus; p. 23 Poet Sage Photos/Shutterstock.com; p. 25 courtesy of The U.S. National Archives and Records Administration; p. 27 (main) Universal History Archive/Getty Images; p. 27 (inset) leezsnow/E+/Getty Images; p. 29 DeAgostini/Getty Images.

Printed in the United States of America

Some of the images in this book illustrate individuals who are models. The depictions do not imply actual situations or events.

CPSIA compliance information: Batch #CS20GS: For further information contact Gareth Stevens, New York, New York at 1-800-542-2595.

Find us on

CONTENTS

Chapter 1: Preparing to Protest.................................4

Chapter 2: Meeting Mr. Madison 8

Chapter 3: Practice Makes Perfect 12

Chapter 4: The First Amendment............................14

Chapter 5: The Second and Third Amendments 16

Chapter 6: The Fourth, Fifth, and Sixth Amendments..............18

Chapter 7: The Seventh Amendment.........................20

Chapter 8: The Eighth and Ninth Amendments 22

Chapter 9: The Tenth Amendment...........................24

Chapter 10: More Amendments.............................26

Glossary 30

For More Information 31

Index..32

WORDS IN THE GLOSSARY APPEAR IN **BOLD** TYPE THE FIRST TIME THEY ARE USED IN THE TEXT.

CHAPTER 1: PREPARING TO PROTEST

Zoe, Gaby, and Will were getting ready to march in front of school. They had made two signs: "Art Is Smart!" and "Music Moves Us!"

"I can't believe our school is cutting art and music classes," Zoe groaned.

"I know," Gaby said. "They're trying to cut costs, but art and music are important!"

"Those are my favorite classes," Will sighed. "This **protest** will show school officials what we think! But . . . I'm worried we'll get in trouble. Aren't you?"

MEET TEAM TIME MACHINE

TEAM TIME MACHINE IS A GROUP OF FRIENDS WHO FOUND A TIME MACHINE IN A VERY ODD LIBRARY. THEY DISCOVERED THAT BOOKS FROM THE LIBRARY COULD POWER THE MACHINE AND TRANSPORT THEM TO DIFFERENT PLACES AND TIMES. IN THIS ADVENTURE, GABY, ZOE, AND WILL LEARN ABOUT THE BILL OF RIGHTS!

"Why would we get in trouble, Will?" Zoe asked.

Gaby added, "It's our right to protest. It's even in the Bill of Rights!"

"Really?" asked Will. "I didn't know the Bill of Rights was for kids."

"It's for all Americans. You really need to stop daydreaming in history class!" Zoe laughed.

"I'd remember more if I learned about it in person!" suggested Will. "Maybe it's time for the time machine?"

"Sounds good!" Gaby laughed. "We do have a test about the Bill of Rights next week. To the library!"

THE BILL OF RIGHTS IS THE NAME FOR THE FIRST 10 AMENDMENTS TO THE U.S. CONSTITUTION, THE HIGHEST LAW IN THE NATION. AMENDMENT MEANS CHANGE OR ADDITION.

THE TEAM FOUND A BOOK CALLED *WRITING THE BILL OF RIGHTS* HIGH UP ON A SHELF IN THEIR AMAZING LIBRARY.

"Are we going back to 1787, the year the Constitution was written?" asked Will. "I remember how much the **Constitutional Convention** argued about adding a list of rights!"

"I remember that too!" Zoe replied. That had been another Team Time Machine adventure. "But James Madison didn't present the Bill of Rights to Congress until two years later."

"So we're going to 1789," Gaby said, "to meet James Madison!"

The kids put the book in the time machine and were soon transported to New York City—June 8, 1789!

JAMES MADISON WAS THE MAIN WRITER OF THE U.S. CONSTITUTION. THE CONSTITUTION EXPLAINS HOW THE FEDERAL, OR NATIONAL, GOVERNMENT SHOULD WORK AND THE DIFFERENT POWERS EACH PART HAS.

The kids recognized Federal Hall from history class. If Congress was meeting, James Madison would be there. They ran inside and stood in a large, crowded hallway.

"So, how do find James Madison?" Zoe asked.

"Perhaps he will find you!" said a voice.

Surprised, Zoe, Gaby, and Will looked up. They saw a man looking down at them curiously.

"I'm James Madison," the man said kindly. "And who might you three be?"

"We meant no disrespect, sir," said Gaby, thinking quickly. "We're just **messengers**!"

JAMES MADISON WAS A MEMBER OF THE U.S. HOUSE OF REPRESENTATIVES, ONE HOUSE OF CONGRESS. HE **REPRESENTED** VIRGINIA.

JAMES MADISON, BORN IN 1751, WAS 38 YEARS OLD WHEN THE FIRST U.S. CONGRESS MET.

CHAPTER 3: PRACTICE MAKES PERFECT

"More messengers!" exclaimed Madison. "Please tell whoever sent you that I'll be ready to present the amendments soon. I just need a bit more time."

"Is there a way we could help, sir?" Gaby asked.

"Truthfully, yes," said Madison. "I want to practice before I speak to Congress. There are a lot of ideas on this list! Perhaps you can listen to them?"

Team Time Machine agreed. They followed Madison into a room filled with papers. They were the first to hear what became the Bill of Rights!

JAMES MADISON DIDN'T THINK A BILL OF RIGHTS WAS NEEDED AT FIRST. HOWEVER, MANY PEOPLE WOULDN'T APPROVE THE CONSTITUTION WITHOUT THE PROMISE IT WOULD BE ADDED.

MADISON USED OTHER WORKS ABOUT PEOPLE'S RIGHTS WHEN WRITING HIS BILL OF RIGHTS. ONE OF THESE WAS ENGLAND'S MAGNA CARTA, WHICH WAS FIRST WRITTEN IN 1215.

MAGNA CARTA

13

CHAPTER 4: THE FIRST AMENDMENT

James Madison began, "One amendment will say that Americans have the right to share ideas in their speech and in the **press**. They can petition, or ask, the government to fix problems. This amendment also protects the right to practice a religion."

"That should be the First Amendment. It's so important!" said Gaby. "Something is missing, though."

"I agree," said Zoe with a smile. "What about a right to gather and protest?"

"Great point!" Madison said. "Americans should be able to gather and ask for changes."

THE FIRST AMENDMENT IS THE REASON WE CAN PROTEST PEACEFULLY AT SCHOOL WITHOUT GETTING IN TROUBLE. WE DIDN'T WANT JAMES MADISON TO FORGET THAT PART!

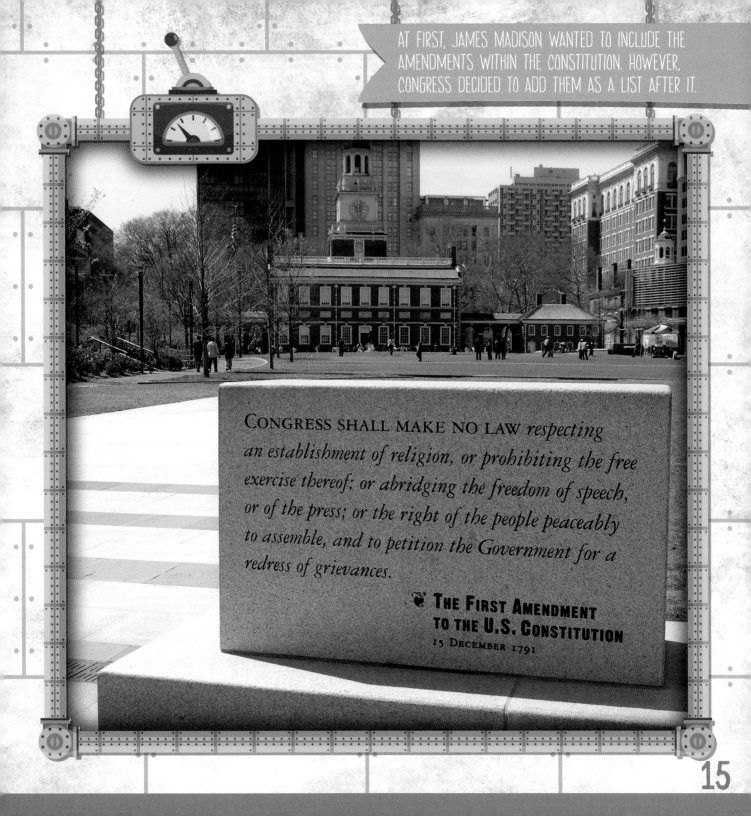

CONGRESS SHALL MAKE NO LAW *respecting an establishment of religion, or prohibiting the free exercise thereof; or abridging the freedom of speech, or of the press; or the right of the people peaceably to assemble, and to petition the Government for a redress of grievances.*

THE FIRST AMENDMENT TO THE U.S. CONSTITUTION
15 DECEMBER 1791

Madison continued with his amendment ideas. They were numbered differently than they are today, but the kids recognized them. They knew that the one that gives people the right to bear arms, or have guns, became the Second Amendment.

The one that became the Third Amendment makes sure people don't have to quarter, or house, soldiers.

"That means you don't have to let soldiers stay in your home," Madison explained. "British soldiers made American colonists house them and feed them before the **American Revolution**."

SOME OF THE WORDS THAT MR. MADISON USED WERE HARD TO UNDERSTAND. THAT'S JUST HOW THEY TALKED AND WROTE BACK THEN. HE EXPLAINED THEM ALL TO US.

TODAY, SOME AMERICANS THINK GUNS ARE TOO DANGEROUS. THEY WANT TO REPEAL, OR END, THE SECOND AMENDMENT. OTHERS ARGUE IT'S A RIGHT THAT SHOULDN'T BE TAKEN AWAY.

Madison explained the Fourth Amendment. It stops the government from searching people and their property and from seizing, or taking, things without a good reason.

"Would someone stealing be a reason to search them?" asked Zoe.

"Yes," said Madison. "Under the British government, officials searched people's homes without a good reason. We don't want that happening again."

The Fifth and Sixth Amendments were next. They provide rights for people who are accused, or blamed, for crimes. They're meant to make the law fair for all.

THE FIFTH AMENDMENT SAYS THE GOVERNMENT CAN TAKE PEOPLE'S PROPERTY, SUCH AS FOR A ROAD. PEOPLE MUST BE PAID FOR IT, HOWEVER.

FIFTH AMENDMENT

- SERIOUS CRIMINAL CHARGES MUST BE STARTED BY A **GRAND JURY**.

- PEOPLE CAN'T BE PUT ON **TRIAL** TWICE FOR THE SAME CRIME.

- THEY DON'T HAVE TO PROVIDE EVIDENCE, OR PROOF, THAT COULD BE USED AGAINST THEM.

- THEY CAN'T BE PUT IN PRISON WITHOUT **DUE PROCESS**.

- THE GOVERNMENT CAN'T TAKE PROPERTY WITHOUT GIVING PEOPLE A FAIR PRICE FOR IT.

SIXTH AMENDMENT

- PEOPLE ACCUSED OF CRIMES MUST HAVE A SPEEDY AND PUBLIC TRIAL.

- THEIR TRIAL MUST BE NEAR THE PLACE WHERE THE CRIME TOOK PLACE.

- THEY MUST BE TOLD THE CHARGES AGAINST THEM.

- THEY MUST HAVE A FAIR **JURY** AT THEIR TRIAL.

- THEY CAN SEE WITNESSES AGAINST THEM AND HAVE THEIR OWN WITNESSES.

- THEY HAVE THE RIGHT TO A LAWYER.

19

CHAPTER 7: THE SEVENTH AMENDMENT

Madison talked about the Seventh Amendment next. He said, "It promises that civil cases in federal, or national, **courts** will have a jury trial."

"What's a civil case?" asked Will.

"They're cases that have to do with arguments between two people or groups," Madison explained. "Usually, civil cases are settled by money. They are different from criminal cases. In criminal cases, the government charges someone with a serious crime such as a robbery. The punishment is often jail."

JAMES MADISON STUDIED LAW, SO HE KNEW ABOUT DIFFERENT KINDS OF COURT CASES. HE BELIEVED A JURY COULD MAKE A TRIAL FAIRER.

THERE ARE DIFFERENT COURTS, INCLUDING LOCAL, STATE, AND FEDERAL COURTS. FEDERAL COURTS SETTLE CASES BETWEEN PEOPLE FROM DIFFERENT STATES OR CASES THAT HAVE TO DO WITH NATIONAL LAWS.

JURY

James Madison explained the Eighth Amendment: "People accused of crimes shouldn't pay an unfair amount of **bail**. They shouldn't pay fines that are too large for lesser crimes. The punishment for a crime also shouldn't be 'cruel and unusual.'"

"Mr. Madison, if a right isn't included in this list, does that mean we don't have it?" asked Will.

"No, I have an amendment here that says just that," Madison replied. "The rights listed here aren't your only rights." That idea became the Ninth Amendment.

PEOPLE ARGUE ABOUT WHAT'S CRUEL AND UNUSUAL PUNISHMENT. IT'S BEEN DECIDED THAT TAKING AWAY SOMEONE'S CITIZENSHIP IS CRUEL AND UNUSUAL, FOR EXAMPLE.

THE U.S. SUPREME COURT HAS THE POWER TO DECIDE IF A LAW OR A COURT RULING GOES AGAINST THE CONSTITUTION. IF IT DOES, IT'S STRUCK DOWN.

U.S. SUPREME COURT BUILDING

The next amendment James Madison talked about became the Tenth Amendment. "The federal government only has the powers in the Constitution," explained Madison. "If a power isn't in the Constitution, it belongs to the states or to the people."

"Why is that one needed, Mr. Madison?" Will asked.

"Many people are afraid our federal government will be too powerful. They worry about people's rights and states' rights. This amendment lets them know that the federal government only has the powers in the Constitution."

PEOPLE ARGUED ABOUT THE POWER OF THE NEW FEDERAL GOVERNMENT UNDER THE U.S. CONSTITUTION. THOSE WHO THOUGHT THE GOVERNMENT WAS TOO POWERFUL WERE CALLED ANTI-FEDERALISTS.

nor shall any fact, triable by a Jury according to *in any Court of the U.S.* the course of the common law, be otherwise re-examinable, than according to the rules of common law.

ARTICLE THE TWELFTH.

where the Value in controversy shall exceed twenty dollars

In suits at common law, the right of trial by Jury shall be pre-served.

ARTICLE THE THIRTEENTH.

Excessive bail shall not be required, nor excessive fines imposed, nor cruel and unusual punishments inflicted.

ARTICLE THE FOURTEENTH.

No State shall infringe the right of trial by Jury in criminal cases, nor the rights of conscience, nor the freedom of speech, or of the press.

dele

ARTICLE THE FIFTEENTH.

The enumeration in the Constitution of certain rights, shall not be construed to deny or disparage others retained by the people.

ARTICLE THE SIXTEENTH.

The powers delegated by the Constitution to the government of the United States, shall be exercised as therein appropriated, so that the Legislative shall never exercise the powers vested in the Execu-tive or Judicial; nor the Executive the powers vested in the Legis-lative or Judicial; nor the Judicial the powers vested in the Legis-lative or Executive.

dele

not a

ARTICLE THE SEVENTEENTH.

to the U.S.

The powers not delegated by the Constitution, nor prohibited by it, to the States, are reserved to the States respectively, *or to the People*

Teste,

JOHN BECKLEY, Clerk.

25

James Madison talked about more amendments that the kids had never heard in history class. He wrote 19! However, they knew all his ideas weren't approved.

When Madison was done speaking, he said, "Thank you for listening and for your helpful thoughts. It's always good to get other people's ideas when creating something so important. I'm ready to present to Congress now!"

"Thank *you*! It's good to know our rights," said Will.

"Remember," said Madison. "These are just *some* rights! Don't forget to use them!"

AN AMENDMENT THAT WASN'T RATIFIED, OR APPROVED, BY THE STATES IN 1789 WAS RATIFIED IN 1992. IT HAD TO DO WITH HOW CONGRESS COULD GIVE ITSELF A RAISE.

JAMES MADISON

27

After James Madison left, Zoe exclaimed, "Wow, we helped write the Bill of Rights!"

"You're welcome, American citizens!" joked Gaby.

"Yeah, but aren't there a lot more amendments?" asked Will.

Gaby said, "In our time, there are 27. People suggest new ones too. It's hard getting an amendment ratified, though."

"Speaking of our time, we should head to the time machine," said Zoe. "Let's get to the school protest and make our voices heard. We can make a difference!"

"Thanks to the First Amendment!" said Will.

NEARLY ALL AMENDMENTS HAVE BEEN PASSED THROUGH ONE METHOD: THE APPROVAL OF TWO-THIRDS OF EACH HOUSE OF CONGRESS AND THREE-FOURTHS OF THE STATES.

JAMES MADISON BECAME THE FOURTH PRESIDENT OF THE UNITED STATES IN 1809.

GLOSSARY

American Revolution: the war in which the colonies won their freedom from England

bail: money given to a court to allow someone to leave jail and return later for a trial

Constitutional Convention: a meeting that took place in 1787 to address problems in the original U.S. constitution, the Articles of Confederation

court: a place where legal matters are talked about and decided on

democratic: describing a form of government in which all citizens participate

due process: the proper way of doing things in a legal case so that accused people's rights are protected

grand jury: a group of people who look at evidence against someone accused of a crime to decide if there should be a trial

jury: a group of people chosen to make a decision in a legal case

messenger: someone who carries notes between two groups or people

press: newspapers, magazines, radio, and TV news

protest: an event at which a group objects to an idea, an act, or a way of doing something

represent: to stand for. A person who represents is a representative.

trial: a meeting in court about crimes or disagreements where decisions are made according to the law

FOR MORE INFORMATION

BOOKS

Chang, Kirsten. *The Bill of Rights*. Minneapolis, MN: Bellwether Media, 2019.

Kawa, Katie. *Bill of Rights*. New York, NY: PowerKids Press, 2017.

Lüsted, Marcia Amidon. *The Bill of Rights*. North Mankato, MN: Pebble, 2019.

WEBSITES

The Bill of Rights
www.ducksters.com/history/us_bill_of_rights.php
Read more about each amendment here.

The U.S. Bill of Rights
www.archives.gov/founding-docs/bill-of-rights-transcript#toc-the-u-s-bill-of-rights
Read the exact language of the Bill of Rights.

INDEX

British 16, 18

Congress 8, 9, 10, 11, 12, 15, 26, 27, 28

Constitution 6, 8, 12, 15, 23, 24

Federal Hall 9, 10

government 8, 14, 18, 20, 24

House of Representatives 10, 25

jury 20

law 6, 18, 20, 21, 23

Madison, James 8, 10, 11, 12, 13, 14, 15, 16, 18, 20, 22, 24, 26, 28, 29

Magna Carta 13

New York City 8, 9

power 8, 23, 24

protest 4, 6, 14, 28

ratified 26, 27, 28

rights 6, 8, 12, 13, 18, 19, 22, 24, 25, 26, 28

states 21, 24, 26, 27, 28

Supreme Court 23

trial 20